handing on the faith

Other ***Handing on the Faith*** titles:

Baptism

RECORD

_____

Child's Name

_____

Parents

_____

Godparents

_____

Date of Baptism

_____

Priest or Deacon

_____

Church

_____

Address

_____

City, State

When You Are a Godparent

Elizabeth Bookser Barkley

ST. ANTHONY MESSENGER PRESS

Cincinnati, Ohio

Nihil Obstat
Rev. Giles H. Pater
Rev. Lawrence Landini, O.F.M.

Imprimi Potest
Rev. Fred Link, O.F.M.
Minister Provincial

Imprimatur
+Most Rev. Carl K. Moeddel
Vicar General and Auxiliary Bishop
Archdiocese of Cincinnati
May 10, 2001

Cover and interior illustrations by Julie Lonneman
Cover and book design by Mary Alfieri

ISBN 0-86716-447-6

Published by St. Anthony Messenger Press
www.AmericanCatholic.org
Printed in the U.S.A.

Contents

Introduction

"I'd like to thank my father, my mother, my god-mother...."

The names went on and on as the young actor rattled off his prepared list of tributes so typical of the movie awards program I was half-attentively watching. It was the mention of his godmother that made me perk up and pay attention.

His godmother: third on the list, right after his parents. Would my godchildren rank me that high—in public acknowledgments, or within their hearts?

How influential am I in the lives of these children, some young adults by now, whose parents have entrusted me with this honor, and obligation? On the day of each Baptism I felt a special bond, but what have I done since then to nourish that bond?

Writing this book has fostered my desire to be a better godmother to my godchildren. In my quest, I have been comforted by several friends who have helped me understand what I feel: humility at being chosen for this role, guilt in knowing that we could stay better connected with our godchildren and their parents, and frustration at the lack of resources in doing so.

When You Are a Godparent is not a foolproof, how-to book. It is an invitation for you to examine the role of godparent, but also to examine your own faith life so you can better model the Christian life to your godchildren as they mature from infancy or childhood into adolescence, eventually embracing their faith as adults.

Just as living the Christian life would be impossible in isolation, so this book would have been impossible without the contributions of faith-filled friends of all ages. They include Leisa Anslinger, Judy Ball, Lisa Biedenbach, Susanne Bookser, Cathy Bookser-Feister, Sister Sarita Cordova, Father Paul Donohue, John Bookser Feister, Bonnie Finn, Julie Loach, Scot Loach, Deb Mato, Dr. James Moore, Sister Fran Repka, Mary Ann Schlomer, Suzanne Schneller, Father Patrick Sheridan and Kim Wilson.

Godparent: A Time-Honored Word

"...In accordance with the view that these persons enter into a spiritual relationship with the baptized person and each other, they were in [Old English] denoted by designations formed by prefixing *god-* to the words expressing natural relationship, as *godsib, godfaeder, godmodor, godbearn,* etc." (From *The Oxford English Dictionary*)

Model, Mentor, Friend for the Journey

If only infants could talk. What would they want from us as godparents? Maybe what an articulate twenty-nine-year-old woman wanted of me when she asked if I would be her godmother:

"I am looking for a godparent who knows the true meaning of compassion and who loves and accepts humankind for what it is," said Kim. "I think the godparent and a godchild should share a strong sense of faith, and have a mutual respect and admiration for one another. To me, my godparent should represent the type of Catholic I want to be."

Well, that's a daunting job description! Maybe it's a good thing that infants and children can't talk. Fortunately for the adult godparent, the infant grows slowly in intellect, emotions and faith. Fortunately, the burden—and gift—of nurturing the faith is not the godparent's alone.

It is the parents, primary guardians of physical life, who take the lead in nurturing the spiritual life within their child. But they need help from godparents and from the broader Christian community.

If parents take seriously their obligation to be the primary teachers of faith, godparents would not be necessary—or would they? Caught up in the here and now of caring for a child—feeding, clothing, educating, transporting, monitoring, mediating—often parents can't find the time or the space, physical or emotional, for faith-focused activities or discussions. Even if parents are so inclined, the child may not be receptive. Often godparents can gently prompt, suggest or just be open to doubts or questions.

In the Czech tradition, Baptisms "are often on the scale of wedding celebrations," says Fran, whose family on both sides is Czech. Parents do not attend the Baptism, giving the godparents an opportunity to bond with their godchild. While the godparents and child are at church, the parents wait and pray at home. It is customary that all the children in the family have the same godparents, so they will remain as a family if anything happens to the parents. "I remember even as a child knowing that if anything happened to Mom and Dad, we would be taken care of by my godparents," she says.

Adults beyond parents are necessary in every child's life, observes the director of formation at a large parish, herself a parent. "Most godparents I meet try to give extra attention, as though all of us seem to realize that children need all the adult support they can have, especially when it comes to matters of faith," Leisa says. "Many of the children I talk to say that their godparent is the one person they've always been able to talk to about God. It seems that the Church has a certain wisdom in asking that we who are parents share our children's faith formation with some other adult(s)."

When I reflect on the influence of my own children's godparents on their lives, I realize that many of the concrete lessons of faith they've learned have been modeled by their godparents.

My godmother has always been a good friend to me, and even though I don t get to see her a lot we have no trouble relating when I do. I guess the important thing is that even when I was a child, she always treated me with respect and made me feel like an adult. A godparent is supposed to be a teacher of life, and how religion fits into life. The best way to teach a child these types of lessons is by example. And the best example to set is by following the most important rule: Love your neighbor as yourself. (Scot, a college student)

It was a godmother who introduced my oldest daughter to a Good Friday tradition in our city: the Way of the Cross and Justice. At that time my two other children were too young to make the rigorous walk to various "stations" along the route under a cold, rainy sky. I was grateful that my oldest daughter could. At her godmother's side, bundled against the cold, she walked, sang and heard stories of modern injustices. Here was an object lesson in Scripture for her: "Blessed are they who hunger and thirst for righteousness, for they will be satisfied" (Matthew 5:6).

Insofar as possible one to be baptized is to be given a sponsor who is...together with the parents, to present an infant at Baptism, and who will help the baptized lead a Christian life in harmony with Baptism, and to fulfill faithfully the obligations connected with it. (From *The Code of Canon Law*, #872)

It was a godmother who broadened another daughter's world and gave her lessons during her formative years about our obligations as the wealthy of the world to care for the poor beyond our borders. Because of my job and family obligations, I could not travel to write of the poor throughout the world, but her godmother did. Birthday and Christmas gifts, bought in Third World countries to help the poor there become self-sufficient, grace my daughter's life as they raise her consciousness. Here was a real life lesson from the Gospels: "Blessed are the merciful, for they will be shown mercy" (Matthew 5:7).

It was a godmother who at every illness or injury, small or large family crisis, or death in the family, seemed to know when to send flowers or a balloon, a stuffed animal, a casserole of homemade food or a card—sometimes hilarious, but always upbeat. Her cheerful deeds were concrete reminders of joy, one infallible mark of a believer: "Blessed are you who are now weeping, for you will laugh" (Luke 6:21).

More lasting than any sermon from the pulpit or lecture from a parent, these godparent moments have threaded themselves through my children's lives. Through their godparents' examples, they have been helped, in the words of Pope Paul VI, to "receive in increasing measure the treasures of the divine life and advance toward the perfection of charity."

On your part, you must make it your constant care to bring her up in the practice of the faith. See that the divine life which God gives her is kept safe from the poison of sin, to grow always stronger in her heart. (*Rite of Baptism*, 56)

Do you not know that all of us who have been baptized into Christ Jesus were baptized into his death? Therefore we have been buried with him by baptism into death, so that, just as Christ was raised from the dead by the glory of the Father, so we too might walk in newness of life. (Romans 6:3-4)

Faith needs the community of believers. It is only within the faith of the Church that each of the faithful can believe. The faith required for Baptism is not a perfect and mature faith, but a beginning that is called to develop. (*Catechism of the Catholic Church*, #1253)

For Reflection and Discussion

Reread the Beatitudes from the Gospels (Matthew 5:3-12 or Luke 6:20-26). Then use these questions to reflect on your life in light of these Scripture passages.

- *Which of the Beatitudes do I already practice in my daily life? Which causes me the most discomfort?*

- *How can I embrace these challenging words of Christ more fully?*

- *What person in my life most embodies the Beatitudes to me? How can I share some of the blessings I've received with this person who is my godchild?*

Launching the Faith Bond

"**G**odparents, are you ready to help the parents of this child in their duty as Christian parents?"

This question, asked in front of all the community assembled at each Baptism, captures succinctly and publicly the role to which you have committed. The initial thrill and pride of being asked to fill this role has passed, and the day has finally arrived when you will enter into a formal bond with a child just beginning a lifelong journey of faith.

The Baptism usually takes place within the context of the Sunday Mass—or at least in the presence of representatives of the Christian community on a Sunday, the day of the week when Catholics renew the Paschal mystery, our redemption from sin and death through Christ's death and resurrection. The celebrating priest or deacon greets the parents and godparents at the entrance of the church or wherever they are waiting with the child. It is here that the congregation first hears the name the child will receive—spoken either by the parents or the godparents. After signing the child's forehead with a cross, claiming the child for Christ, the minister invites the parents and godparents to do the same. From the first rituals of the Baptism, the godparents' role is made clear: they will be the chief support of the parents as the child enters into the mystery of Christ's death and resurrection.

Essential to the Baptism are the readings from Scripture—the regular Sunday readings from the Old and New Testaments within the context of the Mass, or one or two passages from the Gospel, if the child is baptized in separate ceremonies. All are invited to reflect on the words of Scripture and the words of the priest or deacon before joining in the prayers of intercession. Not only the child to be baptized but also the parents and godparents receive the prayers of "the faithful," those who promise to support the child in a life as "faithful follower and a witness" to the gospel.

For the child, the celebrant prays: "Lead her by a holy life to the joys of God's kingdom." This prayer is followed by "Make the lives of her parents and godparents examples of faith to inspire this child."

Soon after that prayer, parents and godparents are asked to present the child for Baptism, being reminded to "make it your constant care to bring him up in the practice of the faith." In the name of the child, the adults publicly renounce sin and evil, proclaiming their belief in the Father, the Son and the Holy Spirit.

Moving to the baptismal font, the godparents sometimes holding the child, they assist the minister as he immerses the child in water, anoints him with holy oil, clothes the child in a white garment, and prays over the ears and the mouth of the child.

Symbolically linking this child's Baptism with

Christ's Baptism, death and resurrection, the minister points to the Easter candle, which burns during every celebration of the Mass. Often it is one of the godparents who lights the baptismal candle as the minister prays that the child may walk in the light of Christ.

This liturgical moment, the one when the child first enters into communion with the larger Christian community, puts the child, parents and godparents in the spotlight. On one level this is most appropriate, since the larger community, witnessing the ceremony, is reminded of their obligation to support not only the infant or child but also the parents. It is the godparents who become symbols of the mission that the whole community must undertake: to support the child accepting the call to "put on Christ."

On another level, the more visible one, the Baptism can deteriorate into a social "event," in which what become most important are the trappings of the day. Much like the Sacrament of Marriage, which often gets buried in the glitz and hubbub of the wedding, the Sacrament of Baptism sometimes drowns in excesses on the part of parents, relatives and friends.

Not that the preparations and rituals aren't important. Attended to with reverence, the details leading up to the ceremony, during the Baptism and at gatherings afterwards can give the message that this sacrament marks the beginning of the child's immersion into a joyful community.

Although participants want the event to go smoothly, in the words of a priest who has presided over many Baptisms, the prepackaged, picture-perfect family and child is mostly a guise that does not communicate the reality of life. Who cares how people look? We should care about what's in the heart.

How can godparents help? By realizing that parents often feel fragile on the day of Baptism. Sometimes this Sacrament of Initiation for their infant or child is a sacrament of reinitiation for parents. They may have been lax in their own pursuit of sacraments and involvement in the life of the Christian community. So when they are asked to speak for their child, to answer "we do" or "we are," they often become painfully aware of the immense responsibility they have assumed with the birth or adoption of a child. In the words of my priest friend, "Sometimes their 'yesses' are really big gulps."

After the Baptism, many families gather for a celebration—often a meal—one that extends the eucharistic celebration. In some families, the godparent plays a special part in these celebrations, acting as host or hostess, or holding the baby while parents greet guests. Some traditions give the godparents much of the spotlight, as they are the ones who present the newly baptized child to the guests.

At the lighting of the baptismal candle, the celebrant prays:

Parents and godparents, this light is entrusted to you to be kept burning brightly. This child of yours has been enlightened by Christ. He is to walk always as a child of the light. May he keep the flame of faith alive in his heart. When the Lord comes, may he go out to meet him with all the saints of the heavenly kingdom. (*Rite of Baptism*, 64)

What mindset can godparents bring to the Baptism, to support the parents that day, no matter where they situate themselves on the continuum of faith?

- A willingness to be open to whatever the day brings, accepting in a spirit of good humor glitches that might be for others cause for distress.

- Acceptance of the moment as it is, choosing to be fully present to receive the graces of the sacrament.

- An attitude of support for the parents, understanding how the reality of Christian parenthood inaugurated at Baptism differs from the gauzy photographs of parents and child on some christening cards.

- A stance of prayerfulness that blocks out the distractions that clothing or gifts can become.

Among many Spanish-speaking people in the United States, the baptismal day is an important occasion, says Sarita, who grew up in the Southwest. The godparents are the main guests for the dinner, held at the home of the newly baptized child. The godmother carries the child into the house and introduces her to every person present, beginning with the mother and the father, then siblings, then other relatives and guests. "The Baptism is a big celebration. It is a happy day," she says.

The Christian community welcomes you with great joy. In its name I claim you for Christ our Savior by the sign of the cross on your foreheads, and invite your parents (and god-parents) to do the same. (*Rite of Baptism,* 41)

I will sprinkle clean water upon you, and you shall be clean from all your uncleannesses, and from all your idols I will cleanse you. A new heart I will give you, and a new spirit I will put within you; and I will remove from your body the heart of stone and give you a heart of flesh. I will put my spirit within you, and make you follow my statutes and be careful to observe my ordinances. Then you shall live in the land that I gave your ancestors; and you shall be my people, and I will be your God. (Ezekiel 36:25-28)

Having received in Baptism the Word, "the true light that enlightens every man," the person baptized becomes a "son of light," indeed, he becomes "light" himself. (*Catechism of the Catholic Church,* #1216)

For Reflection and Discussion

Reread Christ's words from the Gospel challenging his disciples to be the "salt of the earth" and the "light of the world" (Matthew 5:13-16).

- *What talents ("lights") do I have to share with the world?*

- *How can I spread my light rather than hide it "under a bushel basket"?*

- *What "good deeds"—even small ones—can I perform for friends, family or coworkers so I can live up to Christ's challenge that "your light must shine before others"?*

- *Who in my own life has acted as "a light of the world" and a "city set on a mountain" for me? What qualities in that person do I want to bring to my relationship with my godchild?*

Baptism as Gift

Picking a name for a child is often a nine-months' ordeal for parents. They research, negotiate and frequently waffle, sometimes up to the time of birth. Of course at Baptism, especially for a young child rather than a newborn, the name has been worn for a while before it is formally conferred. But a name is the first public gift bestowed on the child at Baptism in the opening words of the baptismal rite as the priest or deacon asks, "What name do you give your child?"

This gift is the first of many this sacrament brings. More importantly, the name symbolizes the birthright the sacrament confers. As a new Christian this child is a member of the Body of Christ. This child is a temple where Father, Son and Holy Spirit abide. At the end of the Baptism, the child will take away a tangible reminder, a gift from the community: the baptismal candle lit from the Easter candle. In some families, this candle remains in a prominent place in the child's bedroom as a symbol of Baptism. Sometimes as other Sacraments of Initiation are conferred—First Communion and Confirmation—

children are asked to find their baptismal candle and to reflect on the newest sacrament in light of their Baptism.

Depending on the family and cultural traditions, godparents and friends shower the newly baptized with other gifts. In some countries, such as Austria, the typical gift of godparent to godchild is a gift of some value, such as a gold spoon or a silver cup. In other traditions, it is the godparents who prepare and serve gifts of food and drink to the parents and guests.

In Ireland, where family ties are strong, the baptismal gown is "treasured and passed on through the generations," says Pat, of Irish ancestry. Whether the child is male or female, the same gown is worn, one symbolic way of keeping in touch with the spirit of ancestors. A friend from the United States reconnected herself with Irish family on a trip to Ireland by searching for her grandfather's name in parish church records from April 1865. "When I found Patrick's name, along with the name of his parents and Baptismal sponsors, I momentarily lost my breath," Judy recalls. "It was a sacred moment. I hope his parents chose good godparents for him, people who helped give him a good start in life and prepared him for the journey he made to America as a young man of eighteen."

One would think that the gift of faith bestowed at Baptism is enough. Not so—because we are human, we need to make concrete our commitment to this new

Christian. "Sacramentals," things associated with the sacrament as a reminder of the graces of the sacrament, have a rich tradition in the Catholic Church. Some sacramentals are not "things" at all. They can be special blessings, rituals, dances, even pilgrimages to sacred shrines or venerated places. Others, such as rosaries or relics, are objects of piety.

One question baptismal sponsors often struggle with is "What kind of gift do I get for my godchild?" This can be particularly difficult if one of the sponsors has not been raised in the Roman Catholic Church or attended a reception where baptismal gifts have been received and displayed.

A rosary, a crucifix, a Bible? These seem most appropriate for the occasion, but just as in a wedding, where the fifth crockpot is about four too many, how do godparents choose a gift that won't be duplicated?

The staff members at most religious gift shops are creative and current in their understanding of the sacraments and sacramentals. And they're eager to give advice. Most have helped other bewildered godparents choose gifts that feel right for them and their godchild.

Since it had been years since I bought a Baptism gift, my friend Suzanne spent several hours with me on a recent trip to her gift shop talking about latest trends and helping me understand the theology of gift-giving. I have culled the following suggestions from her considerable experience and my many hours of delightful browsing. I have eliminated the obvious gifts, such as children's Bibles, crucifixes or plaques. Each category contains general suggestions and some specific suggestions.

Gifts of light

One of the oldest and most powerful symbols associated with the Sacrament of Baptism is light. In the first book of the Bible, we hear the story of creation: "Then God said, 'Let there be light,' and there was light. And God saw that the light was good; and God separated the light from the darkness. God called the light Day" (Genesis 1:3-5).

Candles of all kinds make meaningful gifts. Some contain verses from the baptismal rite or are decorated with symbols of the Christian faith. For godparents with a knack for crafts, the possibilities for a one-of-a-kind candle are endless. Try embedding the birth announcement or a portion of the baptismal rite in the wax. Favorite verses, the child's name and date of Baptism or words related to the godchild's saint can be painted on a candle with poster paint or indelible marker (after wiping the wax with rubbing alcohol). One way for parents to remember the anniversary of their child's Baptism is to light the candle and burn it briefly each year.

Many religious gift shops also carry a variety of nightlights, some more overtly religious (with pictures of Jesus, Mary or angels) and some that would work well as symbols of Baptism (anything related to rebirth in nature, such as rainbows, birds or butterflies).

Gifts of water

Since the essential rite of Baptism centers on water, gifts related to water are rife with significance. For newborns, water gifts can also be gifts to the parents. Many stores, not just religious gift stores, sell small electric fountains

that circulate water and are small enough to fit on a dresser or nightstand. In a nursery, the fountain can serve as a backdrop to calm a restless child or to soothe a frazzled parent. A low-maintenance variation on this water therapy is a tape or compact disc of natural sounds of the ocean or music with water backgrounds. (One of my favorites is a recording that blends seven arrangements of Pachelbel's "Canon" with the sounds of the sea.)

Gifts of nature

The story of the first creation in Genesis is replete with references to nature: "And God said, 'Let the waters bring forth swarms of living creatures, and let birds fly above the earth across the dome of the sky'" (Genesis 1:20) and "'Let the earth bring forth living creatures of every kind: cattle and creeping things and wild animals of every kind'" (Genesis 1:24). For a young child, an age-appropriate living thing is a connection with the rest of God's creation: a fish (another reference to the waters of Baptism) or a low-maintenance caged pet (such as gerbils or a hamster). Be aware that some parents welcome pets (and the accompanying responsibility that their "child's" pet will inevitably bring). For others, another mouth to feed could be the proverbial last straw. Good parent-godparent communication is a must before making such a decision.

An alternative nature gift could be of the floral variety. If weather permits, plant a flowering bush or sapling or some bulbs that will reemerge as a sign of new life each spring. As the child begins to understand the cycle of life, this growing bit of creation will be a visible reminder of the care and attentiveness of godparent to godchild.

Gifts of words

Not everyone loves and appreciates poetry, but if you do, a low-cost gift would be a poem. Try your hand at one in honor of your godchild, weaving in biblical images (light, darkness, water, birth) with homey touches. It doesn't have to be Pulitzer Prize material to touch the parents now and your godchild as she grows.

Or browse through books of poetry to find one that feels right for you and the family. Ones with obvious religious overtones abound, but anything celebrating new life and light might work too, especially if the parents are struggling to reconnect with their own religious beliefs at the Baptism of their first child. (Two of my personal favorites are James Weldon Johnson's "The Creation" and Emily Dickinson's "I'll Tell You How the Sun Rose.")

Many stores carry baptismal remembrance books, with pages to record the date, time and place of the Baptism, and names of parents, grandparents and siblings. In light of the recent wave of creative scrap-booking, a one-of-a-kind baptismal book from a godparent seems within the reach of even those who lack the artistic touch. Leave some pages blank, take pictures and insert them at a later date.

Most gift shops don't carry books specifically geared to the child's Baptism, but many fit with the theme of birth and welcome that the sacrament stresses. Parents will appreciate them now, and children can grow into them.

Of those available now, here are some of my favorites, but more are sure to be published each year.

- *Sleep Sound in Jesus: Gentle Lullabies for Little Ones* by Michael Card (illustrations by Catherine McLaughlin), Harvest House Publishers. This is a book of lullabies and reflections on the lullabies, based on the belief that "at the heart of it all, what lullabies are basically about is *loving*—loving our children and loving God."

- *The Twelve Gifts of Birth* by Charlene Costanzo (photographs by Jill Reger and illustrations by Wendy Wassink Ackison), Featherfew. This book, written for the author's daughters as they approached adulthood, is a book that will appeal to parents now and children as they grow.

- *Tell Me Again About the Night I Was Born* by Jamie Lee Curtis (illustrations by Laura Cornell), Harper Festival. This board book is a delightful narrative of an adopted child's birth.

- *Sister Wendy's Book of Saints* by Sister Wendy Becket, Dorling Kindersley Publishing. Any fan of public television's art connoisseur Sister Wendy won't be surprised at the beautiful classic works of art in color contained and explained in this book.

- *Bible Names for Your Baby* by Joy Gardner and Paul Gardner, The Liturgical Press. The book gives the history of names rooted in the Bible, as well as their meaning in Greek, Hebrew and Latin.

- *Saints' Names for Your Baby* by Fiona MacMath, The Liturgical Press. Each name connects the saint to a feast day, symbol and causes or professions with which they're associated as patrons.

When the godchild is not an infant, but a young child, several books are available to explain the sacrament.

- *When Your Child Becomes Catholic* by Rita Burns Senseman (illustrations by Constance M. Wolfer), St. Anthony Messenger Press, is aimed at parents or godparents who can help their child understand Baptism and other Sacraments of Initiation.

- A helpful book for preschoolers being baptized is *God Makes Me His Child in Baptism* by Janet Wittenback (illustrations by Gordon Willman), Concordia Publishing House. Its explanation of infant Baptism is geared to children ages two to five, but would also be an appropriate gift for siblings of a godchild.

Gifts of music

Music boxes received as baptismal gifts were among my children's favorite keepsakes as they moved through childhood. Some play specifically religious songs (such as *Ave Maria*) but I also recommend any calming song, such as a classic lullaby. One of the bases for selection might be how long the song plays, since parents often wind up the boxes as part of their child's bedtime ritual. Longer-playing variations on the music box are tapes or CDs of soothing music or lullabies.

Gifts to hold

Something for the crib or the rocker is a gift that children and parents will daily associate with the giver. Squeezable toys of biblical characters and washable plush dolls might begin a theme of gifts for birthdays or the anniversary of the Baptism. By the time your godchild begins school, her room could be a haven for such colorful characters as Jonah and the whale, Daniel and the lion, and other Old Testament figures. One of my favorite bears carries the message that is worth reinforcing as the child grows: "God danced on the day you were born."

The blankets one grandmother crocheted for each of my children at their birth soon became an essential part of their comforting routine. Many stores carry small blankets, or throws, with a variety of designs and verses that could help the child remember the special godparent-godchild connection. Some gift shops will embroider details of the Baptism on throws.

Gifts of memory

Frames to hold Baptism photographs come with a variety of biblical texts or baptismal motifs. Have a friend take a picture of you with your godchild (in a christening gown, if you can manage one before the gown is discarded for more comfortable clothes) as a way to mark your special role in his or her life.

Keepsake ornaments announcing the baptismal date, plaques with significant prayers or pictures of the namesake saint, family trees outlining where this child fits in a line of relatives who have also been christened make special gifts.

As toddlers, my children loved looking through piles of cards they were too young to appreciate at Baptism. As I read signatures and notes to them, the cards became a way of keeping alive memories of those who had celebrated their Baptism. As a parent, I would have appreciated a gift to help preserve these cards and notes—a decorated box or a scrapbook. Few parents of newborns have extra time on their hands, so include an offer to assemble the book as part of your gift.

The greatest gift you can give on this day is your supportive presence. Don't worry about the "perfect godparent gift" because there is none. Whatever you choose, make it a symbolic link between you and your new "spiritual relative," the first of many connections you will foster as the years go by.

What name do you give your child?
(*Rite of Baptism*, 76)

But when the fullness of time had come, God sent his Son, born of woman, born under the law, in order to redeem those who were under the law, so that we might receive adoption as children. And because you are children, God has sent the Spirit of his Son into our hearts, crying, "Abba, Father!" So you are no longer a slave but a child, and if a child then also an heir, through God. (Galatians 4:4-7)

God calls each one by name. Everyone's name is sacred. The name is the icon of the person. (*Catechism of the Catholic Church,* #2158)

For Reflection and Discussion

- *Can I build in some time before the Baptism to calm and center myself, so I can bring an attitude of peace to the parents and the child during the Baptism?*

- *Parents of infants and young children need much support as they adapt their lives to a child or work to integrate the youngest into a family with other children. How can I support my godchild's parents during this transition? Consider offering to babysit the child or children while the parents attend Sunday Mass or an evening of renewal. Or, if you live out of town, consider sending a gift certificate for housecleaning or an evening out.*

- *What do I know about the saint for whom my godchild is named? Are there special causes associated with that saint (for example, Saint Francis of Assisi with animals and Saint Elizabeth Ann Seton with education)? If my godchild is not named for a saint, is there a saint who might be of particular interest to the child or family? Is there some meaningful way I can make this connection real to my godchild, even as a young child?*

Keeping in Touch

The Baptism is over, the gifts opened and passed around, the dishes washed and the decorations taken down. The baptismal day has been one of great celebration.

When adults are baptized, the sacrament is the culmination of months of study, preparation, soul-searching and prayer. But when infants and children are baptized, all the preparation is compressed into a short period, during which parents and godparents reflect on why they are bringing this child to the Baptismal font. In the words of the *Catechism of the Catholic Church*, "by its very nature infant Baptism requires a *post-Baptismal catechumenate.*" In other words, now the real work of parents and godparents begins.

Before Acholi children in southern Sudan and northern Uganda are presented at the church for Baptism, they participate in an elaborate name-giving ceremony, according to Paul, who lived in Africa for many years. The newborn is

isolated in the hut with his or her mother and a woman celebrant for several days, then the three emerge for a symbolic tasting of the first human food. Upon shaving the
newborn's head, the celebrant visits grandparents, who
whisper names that the celebrant shares with the mother.
Water saved from the infant's first meal is poured at the
door of the birth-hut, then the mother and child reenter
it. When the celebrant knocks on the door, she asks the
mother the names. Through consensus of those assembled
outside, they arrive at a name, which is announced as the
newborn is carried out of the hut by another
child. "The names given to a newborn
emerge from the significant circumstances surrounding the birth. Each name
bears a personal history," Paul explains.

Just what is this work? Nothing more than helping your
godchild to "put on Christ" as he or she moves through
life. Of course, the parents play the primary role in nurturing the child's faith life. But "god-parents"—parents
on the spiritual plane—also have a unique role in the
child's faith life. Or they should.

Looking back at my own godparents, my mother's
sister and her husband, I don't remember any heart-to-
heart discussions on faith or spirituality. As in many families, my godparents lived miles away—at first within the
same state, and, after our family moved when I was in
second grade, in another state.

So was this relationship special? And, if so, how is it
special? Here is what I remember of my relation to them,

both of whom died before I was a teen.

- Taking a train from our big city to their small town to spend a week with them.

- Being bored because there was no one my age to play with.

- Discovering a vegetable, kohlrabi, which they grew in their family garden, and having the distinction among my sisters of knowing and enjoying some food they had never tasted.

- Exploring their small town—walking "downtown" and venturing out on my own.

- Receiving gifts—not always age-appropriate, but always special, and always sent just to me, not my sisters. (The worst, which I'm sure they chose with great care, was a chocolate, cream and fruit-filled Easter egg; the best, of which I still retain remnants, was a leather-bound manicure kit.)

That I remember these gifts forty years after I received them says much about the impact of our relationship. The other dimension of this relationship I remember is being embraced by their three children, closer to my mother's age than my own. When my cousin and my godmother died, I suspect I grieved more than my sisters, who had not known them on the same level.

Someone recently reminded me that it's not necessary that godparents be pillars of the parish who sit in the first pew, but they must be people who are firmly grounded in their spirituality. My godparents' loving family, where I was welcome and made to feel special, was an extension of my own family's love, another anchor in a time that I was growing into young womanhood.

What makes some godparents memorable, and how can twenty-first century godparents transform this role into a more meaningful one, one that is a vital and not a figurative one?

The key is keeping in touch. The level and manner will vary according to distance between the adult and the child, and the personalities of each.

Sharing presence

In a world that whizzes by so quickly that we often have to stop to catch a breath, what better way to say to a god-child "You're important" than by taking time out of a hectic world to stop in and just "be"? At first, this presence may be more of a gift to the parents than the child. What parent, no matter how wrapped up in the marvel of a new baby, does not long for adult conversation, even if it is conversation about the child? As co-nurturer of the child with the parents, godparents also need to nurture the parents.

A few moments to breathe, take a walk (without an infant in a stroller or other siblings by the hand) will allow parents to jump back into the challenges of parenting with more energy and positive attitudes.

As the child grows, a godparent's presence is even more important. Some young adults I've talked to remember how godparents set aside certain times to be with them. It might be a trip to the zoo, a springtime visit to plant the first flowers of the season together, an afternoon of baking cookies (eating some, delivering others to residents of a nursing home) or watching holiday fireworks.

One thing that stymies godparents is how to turn such events into religious or spiritual moments. Do we have to "talk God"? Anyone who believes in the Incarnation, the event in which God became human in the person of Jesus, won't have to worry about classifying activities they do with godchildren. As theologian Martin Buber has written, "We meet God in the meeting."

When we extend our hand in love and concern to others, when we really listen to them without judging, we are bringing God into our midst. This openness to the other becomes more important as the child hits pre-teen and teen years. I recently read that all teenagers need at least three significant adults in their lives. Why not make the godparent one of them?

Don't forget to be there for the parents during those years of trauma. One mother recalls: "My children's godparents have recognized the role of godparent as a special one with privileges and responsibilities. They have been a special support for me, allowing me to talk freely through issues, such as the choice of a Catholic education, the balance necessary in the practice of Catholicism at home. They have allowed us to grow as a family in faith, respecting us when our practice (and that of our children) has become mystifying to them."

Can this relationship of presence be as strong when miles separate godparent from godchild? In some cases, yes, if there's already a strong relationship between the godparent and the child's parents. Julie, who has lived in Canada much of her adult life, has asked Susie, whom she knew from the States, to be godmother to all five of her children. Susie makes an effort to drive to Canada as often as possible to visit her godchildren. Julie observes,

"She is very special to them and we call her Aunt Susie. They have shared their faith with her."

Lisa, godparent to several children, established a special tradition with her first godchild. When Julie was born, I purchased a nativity set of eighteen pieces. For each Christmas and some other milestones in her life (First Communion and birthdays) thereafter, I gave Julie one piece of the set. By age fourteen, she had all the pieces. She treasures it and looked forward each year to getting the next piece. It was a visual, tangible reminder that she and I are connected through Baptism and that we have a special relationship that goes beyond the Sunday in church when she was blessed with water.

Long-distance connection

Not everyone can be physically present to their godchildren, but the postal service and newer technologies provide efficient links. As children move through the awkward years of puberty, they might be more comfortable not communicating face-to-face, but it's important that godparents not lose contact.

A phone call to mark birthdays or special occasions is a nice reminder of your concern and affection. Young children love to get calls and letters, and teens and young adults rarely mind getting extra attention. Religious gift shops carry cards to mark the anniversary of the child's Baptism, with art and verses to match the child's maturity. I also like the tradition of including references to the child's baptismal name in gifts. If children love books, a bookmark explaining the origin and significance of the name could be included.

If you and your godchild are computer-savvy, E-mail is an excellent (and free) way to keep in touch. Some godparents even have a Web page devoted to their godchildren and update it with notes on family history or special notes on life's milestones.

More sacramental links

Other sacraments seem obvious moments of connection between godparents and their children. Our parish director of religious formation reflects on the importance of reconnecting at these religious landmarks: "When the child approaches the First Eucharist there is a lot of concentration on the circumstances surrounding the child's Baptism, with pictures and baptismal garments and other mementos surfacing. Even with extended families spread apart geographically, it is wonderful that so many godparents are able to come for the celebration."

Many parishes encourage children to repeat not only their baptismal name but also their baptismal sponsor as Confirmation name and sponsor. This repetition stresses the connection between these two Sacraments of Initiation. What a wonderful reminder and wake-up call to godparents that their role as mentor and role model is a lifelong one.

In some families, the traditional bond between godparent and godchild is so strong that even later sacraments, such as Matrimony, highlight that relationship. Fran, a member of a religious community, remembers her godparents talking to her at entrance into religious life and her siblings on their wedding days. Before leaving home for their wedding (or final vows as a sister), Fran says, "the godchild kneels before his or her parents and the godparents stand behind their godchild, hands on each shoulder of the godchild. They instruct the godchild first to ask their parents' forgiveness for past hurts and to ask primarily for their blessing on his/her newly-chosen life."

Forgiveness for the Past, Blessings for the Future

As our godchildren's lives move through their natural ebbs and flows, we can be conduits for them as they reflect on their past lives—with all their failures and successes—and reach out to accept the graces of the present and the future.

Adult sacraments like Matrimony may seem incomprehensible to us as we prepare for the Baptism of an infant or a child. Rooted in today, we may be unable to envision our role decades from now. What is being asked of us in the future is what we are embracing today as we say yes to the invitation to "god-parent" this child. Throughout this child's life, we will model our acceptance of Christ's challenge to "obey everything that I have commanded you" and to be a tangible reminder to our godchildren that no matter what challenges they face in the years ahead we take seriously Christ's words: "I have called you by name" and "I am with you always."

Dear parents and godparents: You have come here to present these children for Baptism. By water and the Holy Spirit they are to receive the gift of new life from God, who is love. (*Rite of Baptism,* 56)

Then Jesus came and said to them, "All authority in heaven and on earth has been given to me. Go therefore and make disciples of all nations, baptizing them in the name of the Father and of the Son and of the Holy Spirit, teaching them to obey everything that I have commanded you. And remember, I am with you always, until the end of the age." (Matthew 28:18-20)

Baptism is the sacrament of faith. But faith needs the community of believers. It is only within the faith of the Church that each of the faithful can believe. (*Catechism of the Catholic Church,* #1253)

For Reflection and Discussion

- *How do I imagine my relationship with my godchild will develop over the years—when my godchild is ten, sixteen, twenty-five? What do I hope to contribute to this person's life?*

- *What traditions can I begin now that we might continue over the years, adapting them as my godchild matures?*

- *One college student, reflecting on his godmother, has said: "My godmother always showed absolute respect to me and everyone else around her, even when not everyone showed her the same respect." What would I like my godchild to say about me when he or she is grown?*

Notes